COLORING BOOK

Country House and Garden

KREATIF LOUNGE

This book belongs to

_____

_____

COLORING TIPS

We have printed the art in single-sided pages. Each image placed on its black-backed page to reduce the bleed-through to the next image.

If you are using markers, strongly recommended sliding a piece of cardstock or the thick paper behind the page you are working on to make sure the ink doesn't stain the next page.

We provided double images placed in version 1 and version 2. Therefore, you will be able to colour your favourite ar ttwice in case you want to have a different version of each artwork.

Now Relax and enjoy the "ME" Time.

VERSION 1

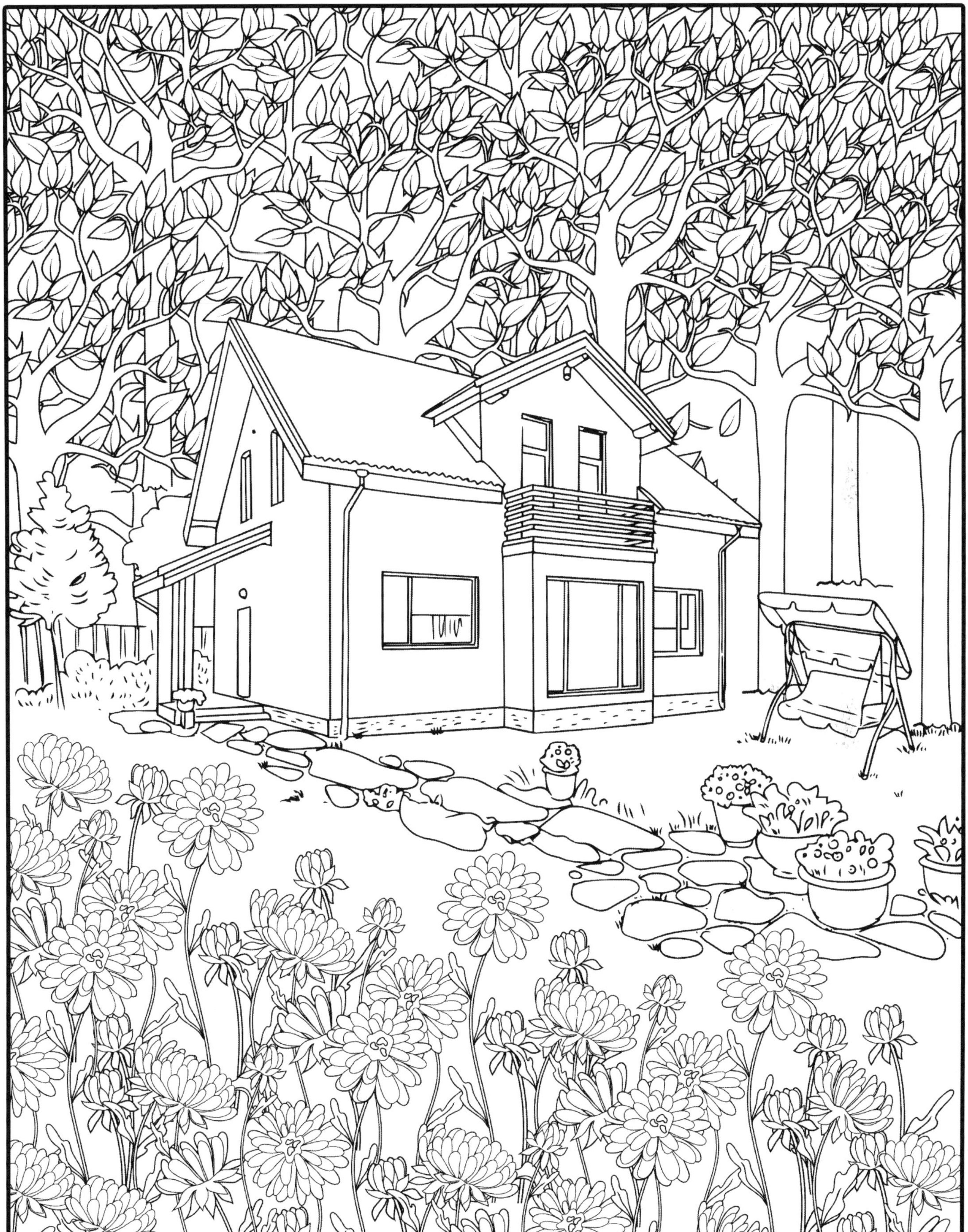

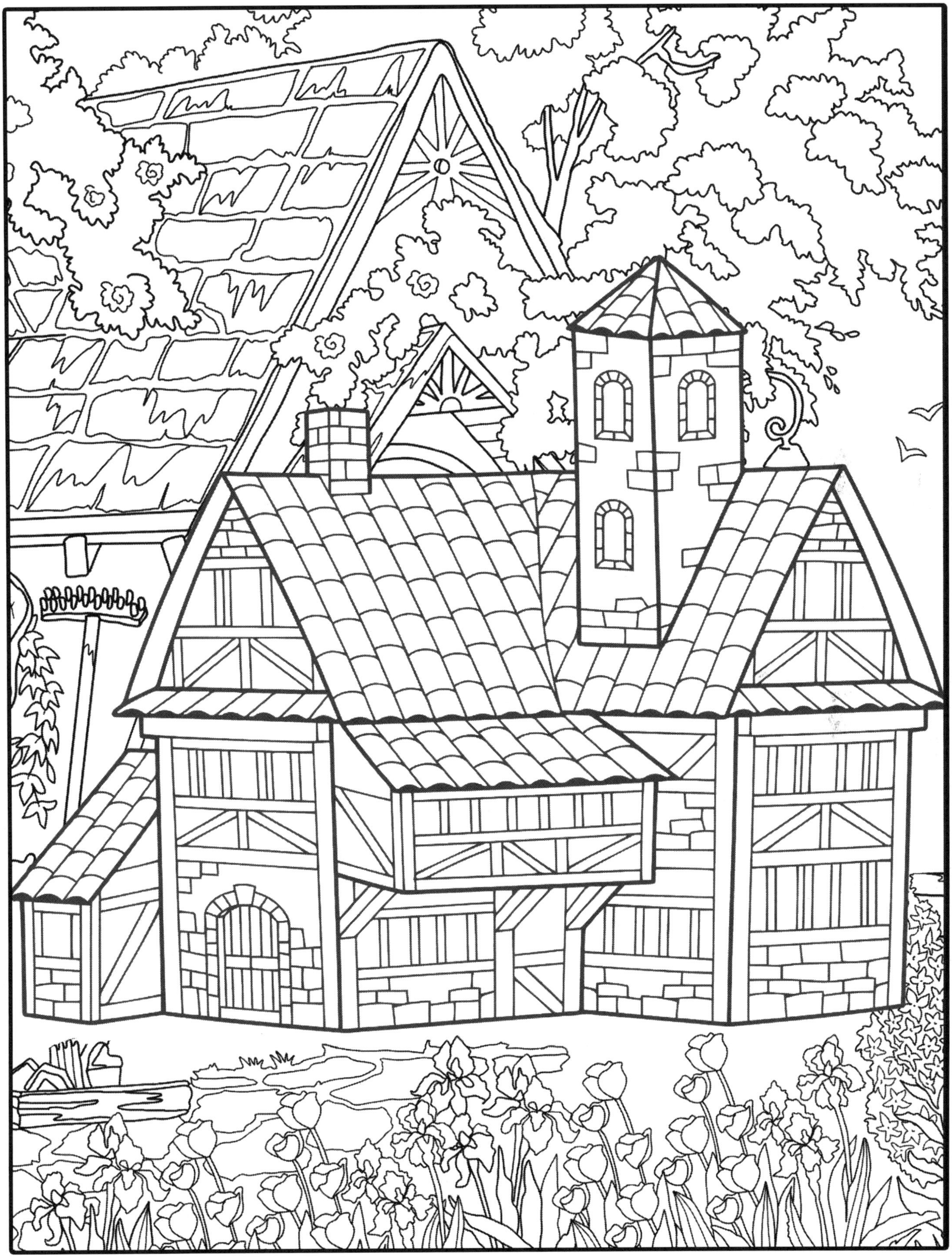

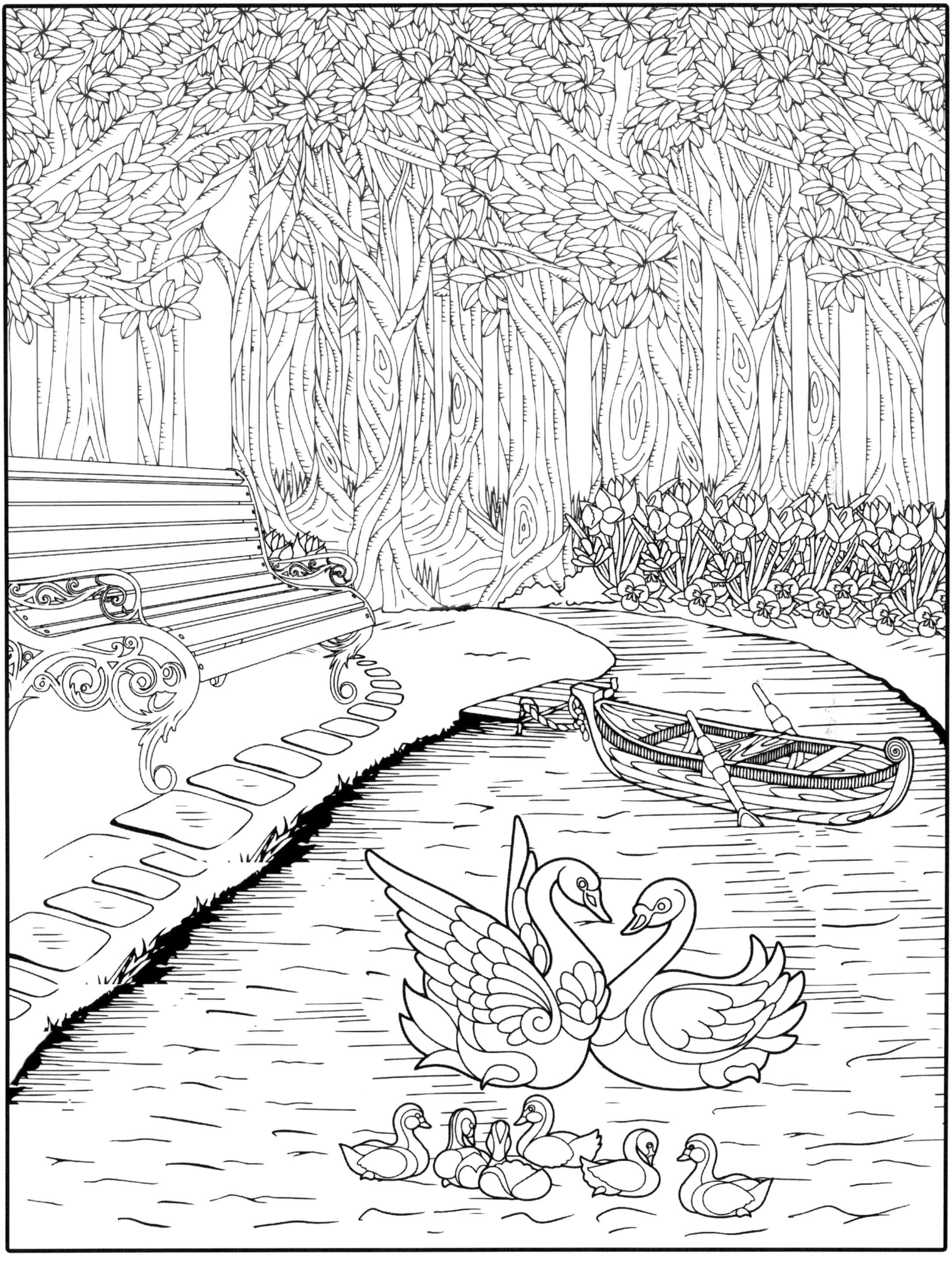

VERSION 2

Made in the USA
Coppell, TX
03 June 2020